IMPROVING LIVES WITH TECHNOLOGY

Kevin Doughty

Andrew Kendall

Foreword

We didn't set out to write a book.

We wanted to tell the story of how Alternative Futures Group and T-Cubed worked over 5 months in 2021 to develop a new model of support for people who have a learning disability.

We shared our story through eight articles on LinkedIn, which also allowed us to summarise our findings.

Positive feedback inspired us to pull these articles together for a wider audience both as an e-book and a paperback.

Our goal is to raise awareness of the potential of technology to improve the lives of people with a learning disability – and share an approach which will deliver better outcomes.

We've added three new chapters. Our introduction summarises current provision and demand, and reviews previous attempts to introduce change through technology.

We've also added a chapter about capacity, consent and the ethics around intrusion and surveillance.

And we've wrapped things up with a chapter that emphasises the need for regular reviews. This chapter also looks to the future of technology in social care.

We hope you enjoy the book. We'd love you hear your views so that we can revise it into a better version that we can offer to all our friends and colleagues throughout the care and support industry.

Acknowledgements

Kevin would like to thank his T-Cubed colleague, Dr Gareth Williams, for his continued collaboration in all matters relating to the role of technology in supporting vulnerable people. Also, Jan Costa, for emphasising the role of informed consent and a robust ethical framework to cover the use of technology, and for challenging his assumptions regarding the benefits of some interventions.

Andrew would like to thank all his colleagues at Alternative Futures Group particularly the wonderful business development team. A special thanks to Carol Toner, Hayley Dale, and Diane Stanley for making our digital pilots happen over the last 12 months. We have learned so much.

Table of Contents

Chapter 1

Introduction

Person-centred lives

People should be at the heart of their own assessment of needs. This allows them to own the process and be confident in the interventions they are offered. This is much better than a support plan which has been put together without input from the person being supported.

Until recently assessments were based on what people could't do, rather than what they could do. This medical model identified deficits which could be targeted and remedied by prescription. This could involve medication but was more likely to involve professional carers taking control.

This approach led to a situation where the needs of people were described by the number of hours when assistance was needed. It invariably required a support worker or a team of support workers who became a blanket of assistance sometimes in place 24 hours a day. Despite the dedication of support workers, opportunities for promoting genuine independence were limited.

To overcome this fundamental limitation, the personalisation agenda has sought to change this method of provision through a series of steps - involving self-directed support, individual budgets, and personal budgets. These culminate in direct payments to service users. This can mean cash that enables the service user to choose and pay for their own services and to employ their own support staff if appropriate.

These steps are shown in Figure 1.1. The assumption is that vulnerable people would be offered advocacy to ensure that they understood the choices, and to ensure that their financial allocations would not be 'wasted' on buying items or services that they may not need.

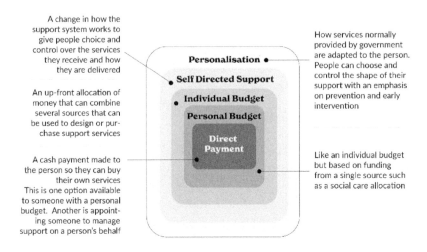

A change in how the support system works to give people choice and control over the services they receive and how they are delivered

How services normally provided by government are adapted to the person. People can choose and control the shape of their support with an emphasis on prevention and early intervention

An up-front allocation of money that can combine several sources that can be used to design or purchase support services

A cash payment made to the person so they can buy their own services This is one option available to someone with a personal budget. Another is appointing someone to manage support on a person's behalf

Like an individual budget but based on funding from a single source such as a social care allocation

Personalisation

Self Directed Support

Individual Budget

Personal Budget

Direct Payment

Figure 1.1: Stages of the personalisation process that can give control to individuals.

The level of payments available for support in the UK depends on the resources available to the commissioners. Contrast this with the situation in some Scandinavian countries where there are no cost limitations following an assessment of need.

Unfortunately, social care in the UK has been historically underfunded. The UK needs better pay rates and a more efficient and effective model of support.

Greater use of technology could save money and create better outcomes. But it will only do this if it is introduced properly and in ways that don't allow technology to take control away from service users.

Figure 1.2 shows how the funding model used to work; it continues to be the basis for assessment employed by many local authorities. It suffers from several short falls:

- The rules linking assessment and a care plan are unclear
- The costs associated with support require people to be slotted into services
- There is little linkage between needs and costs

2

- It stifles innovation and creativity in developing support packages
- The whole process is slow, inefficient, and therefore costly
- It does not tell service users what level of funding is available to them, preventing them from deciding for themselves how they wanted to be supported

Figure 1.2: The 'old' method of calculating a financial allocation.

To address these issues, a new way of deciding openly how much money an individual would be entitled to as an individual budget was created. It was known as a Resource Allocation System (RAS), and it was introduced several years ago to provide a fairer and more reasonable level of financial support by:

- Providing support wherever possible to remove or reduce the level of help that will be required in the future as a means of increasing independence i.e., promoting the principles of **prevention**
- Offering enough money to enable the person to become (or continue to be) a full and active citizen i.e., establishing the principle of **sufficiency**
- Making sure that people with similar needs for help should receive similar levels of money i.e., supporting the principle of **equity**
- People should receive no more support from the system than is necessary to enable them to be full and active citizens i.e., enabling people to contribute **to their own care** (and exercise more self-care)
- Encouraging people to pay for their own support, but not to such an extent that they are discouraged from earning or saving for themselves i.e., preventing **poverty**

3

The process shown in Figure 1.3 represents a radical change to resource allocation that should enable more self-assessment of needs in a way that reduces transactional costs, and which provides fairer and more transparent funding.

This should enable more forward planning to be performed giving users the confidence to use more indirect forms of support, thus reducing their reliance on paid support staff.

Although the principles were introduced in 2003 but extended through different pilots and framework developments, they have yet to be universally accepted across different user groups. Indeed, several different approaches are taken:

- A linear approach, converting assessment points to funding allocations with a standard amount of funding available per point
- A super-linear approach recognising that care costs increase rapidly for more complex cases, including many people with a learning disability
- A banded approach to differentiate between users who have more 'standard' and those who have more complex needs
- A group approach which uses a different scheme for different user groups for whom costs have traditionally been higher

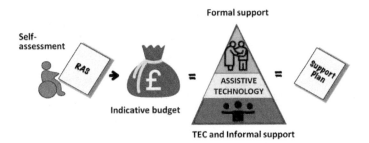

Figure 1.3: An approach to support plans based on a resource allocation system.

The fundamental differences between the old and the new schemes are:

- A greater use of self-assessment – though often supported by different advocates or family members
- The principle of replacing the number of hours of support with a support plan consisting of an individual number of (paid) support hours, plus technology (Technology Enabled Care applications and equipment) and help from family, friends, and other more natural sources such as community groups

Formal support can be split into one-to-one hours, overnight (sleeping) support, day-care centre attendance, or activities such as attending leisure events or activities. The key was to break away from the old way of developing a care plan on behalf of an individual with needs, to coproducing a more flexible support plan with the service user. This could have, and perhaps should have, led to a rapid growth in the use of assistive technology within support plans. However, the move away from support hours to more flexible support plans has been extremely slow in some areas, especially in shared housing where support resources are currently shared between the residents, irrespective of their individual needs.

The use of technology has also been hindered by a lack of appropriately evidenced technology interventions and by a risk-averse culture in many organisations.

Despite a general improvement in the reliability and aesthetic appearance of many technology products, most adults with learning disability continue to be supported in the same ways as ten years ago. Digital technologies and ubiquitous consumer devices may be a catalyst for change that is ripe for introduction.

The New Care Act

The English (New) Care Act 2014 sets out local authority responsibilities relating the assessment of people's needs and their eligibility for publicly funded care and support.

It follows previous attempts to introduce Person Centred Care by placing specific requirements on local authorities that will be relevant to all citizens including those who are disabled and those who are already in the social care system. The responsibilities are:

- To carry out an assessment of anyone who appears to require *care and support*, regardless of their likely eligibility for state-funded care
- To focus the assessment on *the person's needs* and how they impact on their *wellbeing*, and *the outcomes they want to achieve*
- To involve the person in the assessment and, where appropriate, their carer or someone else they nominate – **nothing about me without me**
- To provide access to an independent advocate to support the person's involvement in the assessment if required
- To consider *other things besides care services that can contribute to the desired outcomes* (e.g., preventive services, community support)
- To use a **strength-based approach** to help individuals to deal with life's challenges in achieving their desired goals and outcomes.

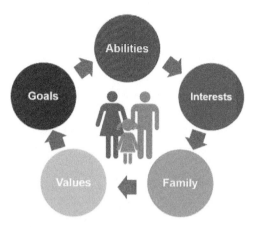

Figure 1.4: Considering the strengths of the individual in assessment.

The focus of the Care Act is on a better assessment of needs that genuinely places the individual at the centre of the approach, and which considers factors shown in Figure 1.4

The assessment process aims to find out what the person themselves wants to achieve a good or a better life for them (and for their family). They might also be able to explain how they believe that a care organisation can work with them to achieve their aims. This is decidedly different to an exercise in finding their deficits and trying to compensate for them by putting in place a service that will do things for them or instead of them because they are unable to do things for themselves. Rather, it focuses on what they can do, and how they might be supported to move forward, perhaps through relatively small steps, towards their objectives.

Thereafter, the task is to use a combination of the available intervention resources to meet these needs in a support plan, which can be explained to the service user (and to his/her advisors) in such a way that they understand how they can choose different elements as appropriate. This new approach is expanded in Chapter 4.

The collection of information, sometimes called profiling (or our preferred expression – discovery), involves open questions (rather than a tick-box approach) in line with the principles of person-centred assessment and care.

Assessors often need to check that they have collected the correct information by presenting the answers back for confirmation. The process should identify the potential for improving the individual's life through a series of interventions i.e., the support plan.

This should be rather more than the number of hours of support needed, and should include opportunities to use more informal support, as well as an extended use of assistive and information technologies. This could form a blended approach which includes the use of technology applications, as will be discussed throughout this book.

A failure to appreciate the potential for using 'lighter touch' interventions, especially more assistive technologies, and consumer products, means that opportunities to use more standard gadgets in all aspects of life are being missed. It also perpetuates the old model of care that limits independence.

There are therefore three main challenges to address:

1. Defining the overall needs through a relatively small number of attributes which remain personal despite having universal application

2. Developing a method of linking the needs to some relevant technology (or lighter touch) intervention options without being prescriptive

3. Monitoring the use of the technology applications and the success in achieving the required outcomes and goals

Summary of Following Chapters

The rest of this book consists of ten chapters:

Chapter 2 - Describes how consumer technologies and devices are all around us and can be repurposed to improve lives on an individual basis that overcome many of the cost constraints and the stigma associated with the use of specialist assistive technologies. It introduces our new model of support based on AT, IT, and care

Chapter 3 - The obstacles that prevent individuals from fulfilling their potential are discussed in terms of the Maslow Hierarchy of Needs and the Sailboat metaphor of Kaufman. A new metaphor – the Tree of Life – is introduced which enables both growth and security needs to be described in ways that are relevant to a technology enabled life.

Chapter 4 - The principles of person-centred assessment are described, with examples of how a strength-based approach can be used to enable an individual to achieve some of their goals and ambitions through a series of steps.

Chapter 5 – Considers the importance of good communication to our well-being, especially during a lock-down where friends, family and support workers may need to link using technology. It considers the emerging roles of video calls, social media, and eSports in keeping people engaged and in touch

Chapter 6 - The importance of keeping people safe and managing risk is introduced. The need for technology interventions to help with behavioural issues as well as those relevant to the environment, physical health and mental health are considered. A role for new activity monitoring systems is highlighted.

Chapter 7 - Introduces the need to fully evaluate technologies in terms of which needs they can or can't address. A comparison is made between traditional assistive technologies and repurposed consumer devices including smartphones and apps. A technique is developed which enables all devices to be described in terms of their success in addressing the needs of individuals using an expanded form of the Tree of Life metaphor.

Chapter 8 - We describe the development of an end-to-end service to deliver technology solutions. This includes a focus on the process for matching needs with technology applications to optimize the solutions and the outcomes. Different products are compared using this approach. The importance of partnerships in delivering the service is emphasized.

Chapter 9 - This chapter considers vignettes of two people who are living with a learning disability in the community. It describes how specific technological interventions can improve their respective qualities of life, and outcomes.

Chapter 10 – As the potential of activity monitoring, smart sensors, and smart home technologies to monitor and control our lives increases, we introduce a note of caution. This takes the form of a discussion on ethics which highlights the need to consider and address the views of service user, especially if they have the capacity to understand the possible impact of technology on their lives.

Chapter 11 – Conclusions – The need to review technology interventions is discussed, and a methodology proposed. The chapter ends by considering possible future changes in social care resulting from new developments in IoT, soft robotics and wearable devices.

Chapter 2

Technology is all around us - Let's use it to improve lives

Introduction

To paraphrase John Donne and The Beatles, nobody can live an entirely independent life - we all need a little help from our friends, families, and carers. And some people need extra help to manage routine domestic tasks. This used to be called "physical help from other people", which usually meant family and friends helping an individual to perform various tasks. More recently, this help has been provided by professional carers or support workers, especially for people without informal help.

But this definition of help is too narrow. Why should people depend on others - usually strangers - to enable them to live well in the community? Can technology help alongside (or perhaps instead of) conventional help?

The answer is yes: technology can help in a big way. But this potential can only start to be realised if we recognise that technology is now part of everyday life, and that it is no longer stigmatizing, expensive and "uncool".

Raising awareness is the starting point for improving lives using a combination of Information Technology (IT), Assistive Technology (AT) and conventional care and support. This "hybrid" concept has been developed by T-Cubed and Alternative Futures Group (AFG) during the early months of 2021.

We begin by showing how gadgets, gizmos and personal consumer devices are already fundamental to how we live. We'll then use these items as a platform on which to grow an expanded range of service interventions that can support an increasing number of the needs that face people with disabilities.

The right combination of technological interventions and more conventional support can improve the lives of thousands of people. The challenge is to match peoples' needs to the intervention within a service proposition, in such a way that the user can exercise choice. Any approach must also recognise that peoples' needs and preferences and the capabilities and limitations of technology change over time.

The approach that we outline in this book represents a cultural shift: one that needs to occur across the care and support sector from the sharp end of service delivery, to those who decide on policy, to those who ensure quality outcomes.

Let's begin with a day in the life of a graduate called Steven. Steven is 26 and lives on his own in an apartment in the middle of a Lancashire town. That's all we need to know for now.

Steven's morning routine

Steven needs to wake up at 7.30am to go to work. He has a smartphone which he uses to manage much of his life. He also has some smart gadgets, all of which he can manage through apps on his phone.

Figure 2.1 shows his alerts and action every weekday morning. His alarms work through his Amazon Echo device which plays him music or the news, switches on his bedside lamp, and interacts with his Hive thermostat to make sure the boiler is working, and the temperature in the bathroom is a comfortable 24^0C.

Figure 2.1: Standard Devices Used to Help Steven Get Up in the Morning

Steven's breakfast routine

Steven relies on technology to help him make breakfast. He loves 2 cups of coffee while he watches Breakfast TV. He either has some toast or some warm croissants before loading the dishwasher, brushing his teeth and going to work. Figure 2.2 shows his kitchen appliances.

Figure 2.2: Steven's Kitchen Appliances

Steven's journey to work

After passing his driving test, Steven bought a car which he uses so he doesn't have to wait for a bus in the rain. He has a Tile device attached to his keyring so that he doesn't lose time trying to find it when he's in a hurry. His car has a first-class music system that links to his smartphone, enabling him also to make or accept calls handsfree while driving.

He also used a GPS guidance system to ensure that he doesn't become lost if he misses a turning, a dash-cam to record other traffic in case of incidents, and a set of parking sensors to help him to park neatly in the tight spaces in his works car park. These are shown in Figure 2.3.

Figure 2.3: Consumer Devices to Simplify Steven's Journey to Work

Entertainment, Cooking and Keeping His Apartment Clean

Steven has access to Netflix, and he enjoys time in front of his large TV, which he also use as a monitor for his games console. He considers himself a good cook, and a bit of a geek in terms of the appliances in his kitchen. He has an air-fryer, an internet-linked fridge and a washer-dryer than can be controlled using his smartphone. These are shown in Figure 2.4, which also shows the robotic vacuum-cleaner that he uses to clean the floors while he's out at work.

Figure 2.4: Steven's Gadgets that Support His Modern Lifestyle

Who is Steven?

Steven is an intelligent young man who values his independence, his ability to enjoy his life using all the technologies that are available to him, subject to his income. We all probably know, or are related to, someone like Steven.

But Steven could be a high-functioning individual on the autistic spectrum, and who struggles to perform routine tasks and to manage schedules without regular prompts and reminders. People with similar issues might not be able to live independently, hold down a regular job, and manage domestic tasks. They could become a burden on their families and on society, failing to achieve their potential.

Consumer technologies can help someone to live a full and 'normal' life. The challenge is to identify individual needs, and to suggest a personalised, hybrid of smart devices and conventional training and support that addresses issues in ways that are acceptable and appropriate for Steven, or for someone like him. This isn't trivial, but it can be achieved through a new approach to assessment within a new service proposition.

The following chapter will describe a framework of assessment and interventions that will enable the use of technology within a service that will benefit people with a wide range of learning disabilities and/or mental health issues.

Chapter 3

The barriers to increasing the use of technology to improve people's lives

Introduction

Many support services aim to help people thrive rather than simply to survive, especially if they are challenged by disabilities of any form. Maslow introduced his hierarchy of needs to describe motivation in several steps. These are often described in an ascending order of needs, the idea being that individuals can only move up the steps when they have achieved the previous level:

- Physiological
- Safety
- Love/belonging
- Esteem
- Self-actualisation

The hierarchy has been used to describe the types of care needs that individuals can be supported with to help them fulfil their potential. One of the authors (Kevin) extended this model to indicate how assistive technologies can be used at each level of the hierarchy. Commissioners have mainly focused on the lower levels of the hierarchy, often at the expense of the higher ones. This is sometimes because of financial constraints.

Everyone's needs are different at each level of the hierarchy - and these needs can often define peoples' lives. The fulfillment of needs is often limited by other factors including levels of disability (such as sight and speech) and by environmental factors (such as living conditions and access to educational aids, IT systems and specialist support). We think there should be a better way of thinking about needs that gives equal emphasis to higher level needs as to those that are related to health and safety. Such an approach may be fundamental to a strengths-based approach.

Kaufman's sailboat metaphor, shown in Figure 3.1, improves on Maslow's hierarchy by introducing the sails as the growth element which can be unfurled to provide the energy to go anywhere and to achieve anything – but only if the hull has no holes. These two parts combine to provide the flexibility to deal with interactions with other boats, and to adjust direction and ambition when the winds and the tides are driving change.

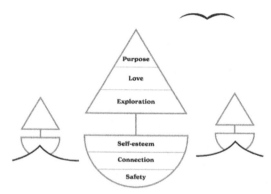

Figure 3.1: The Kaufman Sailboat Metaphor

The Tree of Life Metaphor

We've enhanced the Sailboat metaphor to address a wider set of connected needs. This uses the root structure of the tree to provide the foundations which are firmly embedded in the soil. Growth is represented by the solid boughs which branch off the trunk, which then support the twigs and then the buds and leaves. The trunk allows sap to run from the roots to the branches and represents the need for good communication and connections.

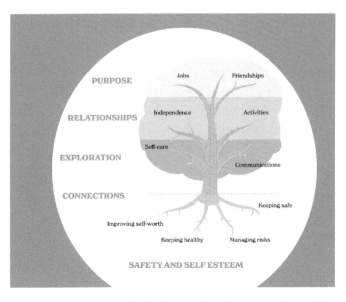

Figure 3.2: A New 'Tree of Life' Metaphor for Growth and Security

The growth of a tree may be restricted by several factors. Wind, frost, and other environmental elements can be a major problem as can the lack of water, and nutrients in the soil. The sun and rain can help overcome these issues in the same way as support staff, training, access to technology, and emotional help and encouragement may be essential to fulfil an individual's ambitions.

Technology Barriers

Many people already see high quality broadband as a utility that enables education, connection, entertainment, and modern living. Poor access to broadband is a barrier to services that rely on the Internet, as is a lack of equipment in the home that can take advantage of digital communications. Providing everyone with the most appropriate devices to meet their needs and abilities would ensure that more vulnerable people could share the benefits of technology and make use of consumer devices of the type described in Chapter 2.

The practical use of technology depends both on knowing which applications are relevant, useful, and usable and being able to employ them consistently over an extended period. Suggestions can be part of a modern assessment process which is backed up with the necessary training in their use. For people with a learning disability, the training must include the support workers who help people to achieve their ambitions every day. Everyone needs to develop the digital skills that are fundamental to expanding the use of technology. There needs also to be 24-hour support for the technology, so that users are not left unable to use their devices and applications in the event of a problem with their equipment or with their broadband.

Physical Barriers

Some disabled people need to overcome physical, health and sensory issues as well as those relating to cognition. Digital technologies were once designed only to meet the needs of people who love technology and are comfortable with it. Instructions were poor and things were fiddly, often needing to be switched off and restarted. They relied on the dexterity, good eyesight, and perfect hearing of the users.

Fortunately, digital accessibility has improved immensely in recent years; designers have appreciated the benefits of universal design principles. Voice interactions have helped to overcome the need to be able to read small print and to type at a keyboard. And websites now make better use of colour and offer the means to increase font size.

Figure 3.3: Assistive Devices to Overcome Sight, Hearing and Communication Issues

The examples of assistive technologies shown in Figure 3.3 can help people with sensory and communication disabilities to use consumer devices more easily. The Orca device on the left attaches to spectacles and can identify signs, characters and colours while the Pebbel screen expander helps users to read computer screens. The Nuhera IQbuds provide personalised hearing amplification. The symbol to speech converter enables users to interact with voice assistant devices such as the Amazon Echo to control their environment.

Conclusions

When an individual's needs have been identified, a combination of training and technology can combine to give anyone access to the digital equipment that can make a difference to their lives.

Consumer devices can often perform the heavy lifting associated with improved care and support They may need to be introduced alongside other assistive technologies that can help overcome barriers that may prevent them taking full advantage of the potential of the consumer devices.

Assessments need therefore to be holistic and identify those obstacles, and then recommend other technologies that can overcome these hurdles and help to access them.

This requires a service-based approach which we will present in succeeding chapters.

Chapter 4

Using a strengths-based approach to achieve personal goals

Introduction

The Care Act of 2014 attempted to change the focus of assessments from the old medical model that addressed dependencies and deficits to one that is person-centred that looks at how outcomes and quality of life can be improved. The assessment approach can be summarised by Table 4.1.

Table 4.1: Principles of Person-centred Assessment

is...	is not...
Person-centred	Practitioner-based
Strengths-based	Problem-based
Skills acquisition	Deficit focus
Collaboration	Professional dominance
Community integration	Acute treatment
Quality of life	Cure/improvement
Community-based	Facility-based
Choices	Dependence
Least restrictive	Episodic
Preventative	Reactive

Strengths-Based Considerations

Everyone is different. And we live in different environments that can affect how we develop and mature in life. To take a person-centred approach to assessment and intervention, we must focus on identifying the strengths and assets that people have as a platform for improving lives.

Figure 4.1 shows the eight principles of a strength-based approach which should underpin the assessment process and help to establish those things that need to be done or changed to move towards achieving the desired outcomes or ambitions.

Figure 4.1: A Strengths-based Approach to Assessment

Examples of Goals and Ambitions

People who have a learning disability may wish to do many things for themselves ranging from being able to travel on their own, to attending college, through to holding down a regular job and getting married. This involves learning some specific life-skills as well as overcoming some of the obstacles they will face. These ambitions need to be broken down into several small steps, each of which represents a skill to be learned – often with help from others.

Figure 4.2 shows the steps that may be needed to achieve someone's personal goal of going to college and achieving a pass in a cookery course:

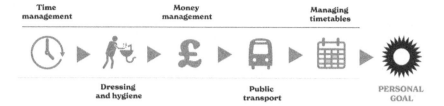

Figure 4.2: Steps to Achieving a Qualification and Training Goal

Developing a New Circle of Support

Personal goals can only be achieved with the support of an individual's entire circle of support. In the example of Figure 4.2, friends, family, college tutors and support workers can all play an active part in developing the skills needed to achieve the goal.

Many of these steps also involve the use of technology. For example, time management could make use of an app such as Timely, Harvest or Remember the Milk, whereas computer-based systems such as Planday or Roubler enable timetables to be printed out at home.

Similarly, there are smartphone apps to help with travel on public transport, which make use of GPS for location support. An example is the Way2b app works with a linked smartwatch to give directions. These all rely on computer systems and information technology to help develop the skills needed to make the small steps towards a bigger goal.

There remain several roles for families, friends and support workers including the understanding of money, and reinforcing the values of society in everything that people do. But when information technology and human support aren't available, there are also bespoke assistive devices that can provide personalised support. For example, the Abilia Memoplanner can be used as a calendar for emphasising tasks and time keeping, or personal voice assistants can provide timely messaging.

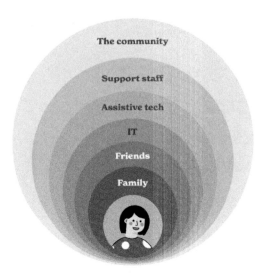

Figure 4.3: An extended Circle of Support

Individuals can build an extended circle of support around themselves, as shown in Figure 4.3. It can be used to focus on the strengths of each of the circles, starting with the person themselves, and identifying and promoting their existing skills and capabilities. It allows the roles of family members and friends to be enhanced so that they can be empowered to play more active roles.

The new circles of support provided by Information Technology (IT) and by Assistive Technologies (AT) enable new and exciting ways to encourage independence. IT is a not only a subject taught in schools, but something that everyone uses in their everyday lives; it would be wrong not to include it as a tool of support. AT can be more bespoke but when it includes everything from walking aids to spectacles and hearing aids, it is apparent that it can provide easy to use compensation for any physical or cognitive issue.

Conclusions

A strengths-led approach to supporting more independence through achieving personal goals lead naturally to the development of an extended Circle of Support model. This extended model makes use of Information Technology and Assistive Technologies where these are appropriate. To make best use of IT and AT we need an assessment that focuses on addressing needs using a strengths-based approach.

In the next chapter, we will look at how vulnerable people can enhance their communication and connections using technology.

Chapter 5

The Role of Smart Devices in Addressing the Communication Needs of Vulnerable People

Introduction

Good communications help people connect with friends, family, and others in their community groups. During the long days of lock-down many vulnerable people had to be shielded. Some went many months without meeting their families and friends.

The problem was partly solved using the telephone using either a landline or, increasingly, a mobile phone or smartphone. But many properties no longer have a landline, due to high costs. And some of the most vulnerable people either don't own a mobile device or they've not been shown how to use it. The lockdown situation highlighted the importance of communication, and that many people struggle to connect for one reason or another.

In this chapter, we describe how smart technology devices can help people connect using digital techniques that are efficient, low-cost, and highly usable.

Special telephones

It is nearly 150 years since Alexander Graham Bell invented the telephone. It transformed how people connected, slowly replacing the use of smoke signals, morse code, homing pigeons and letter writing. The need for wires and telephone exchanges, together with relatively expensive line rentals, limited access for the first 100 years to business and the middle classes.

There are now handset designs and gadgets that are suitable for people with disabilities including amplifiers, loud ringers, text telephones, units for people with larynx issues, ring signaling devices such as light flashers and bed-shakers.

A range of useful assistive devices is shown in Figure 5.1. They enable people with hearing impairments to make use of telephone systems and to engage with family and friends irrespective of distance. It should be remembered that people with a learning disability can also have a hearing impairment that can significantly impact on their ability to communicate and to socialise.

Figure 5.1: Specialist Telephone Devices and Equipment for People with Hearing Loss

Modern mobile phones and smartphones have features that help people with a hearing loss. Some mobile phones are designed with such users in mind. These include the devices shown in Figure 5.2 and the Bluetooth accessories on the right of Figure 5.2 that enable remote notification and the amplification of calls.

Figure 5.2: Mobile phones and accessories for people with hearing loss

One advantage of smartphones is the use of apps, which include a range that are designed to help people with hearing loss in their daily lives. Both Android and iPhones have basic sound amplifier functions (the Live Listen option) but both types of smartphone can be used with the following apps:

1. Ava - an instant transcription app for the words of a group of people. It allows people who are deaf or hard of hearing to distinctly follow a conversation within a group without having to lip-read. Ideal when people are wearing masks.
2. TapSOS - this allows deaf and hard of hearing person to connect with emergency services in a nonverbal way. When connecting, the app pinpoints the exact location and send all the data stored in the user's profile in seconds.
3. RogerVoice – this offers a live transcription of telephone conversations in more than 100 languages, as well as the option of answering by voice synthesis.
4. Subtitle Viewer – this uses the smartphones' microphones to offer the possibility of viewing subtitles in different languages live on the user's phone, synchronized with television or cinema films.

Visual communication

Fast digital communications, together with the cameras included on every smartphone, tablet device and laptop, has helped video communications to boom in recent years. The dedicated videophone has been consigned to the scrap heap of history.

Being able to see a person during a conversation has enriched communication and has brought virtual presence closer to reality. Although hand-held devices are ideal for one-to-one conversations, and for keeping in touch with loved ones, opportunities for improving the connections benefit from fixed devices and larger screens. These are much better for online training and allow for more comfortable viewing.

Figure 5.3: Popular TV-based Video Communication Interface Systems

The television continues to dominate most living rooms so it is not surprising that it can - by the addition of a webcam or dedicated set-top box - become the visual interface of choice.

During the pandemic, versions of Portal that plugged into a conventional TV soared. These have a camera system that tracks movement, enabling them to be used while the user walks about the room. Care Messenger supports a similar approach with the advantage of providing an interface for providing reminders. Kraydel uses the TV both to provide video conferencing and as the hub for more advanced activity monitoring and support applications. These three examples of TV-based video communication systems are shown in Figure 5.3.

An alternative to using the TV is to repurpose other consumer devices for video calling. Most tablets can be used as large mobile phones that enable popular group chat applications such as Messenger and WhatsApp which have end-to-end encryption. However, standard devices can be difficult to manage without considerable technical support - although large iPads and Android devices have enjoyed considerable popularity with older users whose eyesight may not be suited to phones and smaller tablet devices.

One approach is to use a 'walled garden' which overcomes many navigation issues by presenting users with a simplified user interface; this can avoid the need for passwords and offers the advantage of always being left on. It also opens up the potential for using remote consultations with professionals and for reducing the incidence of social isolation or feelings of loneliness.

Similar benefits can be obtained by repurposing other touch-screen devices such as the Amazon Echo Show series and the Google Hub to provide the video interactions using existing contacts. These devices can also be used for news alerts, medication reminders, playing music on demand and for controlling smart home devices. There are many available devices and applications that can encourage video interactions for those people who crave enhanced interactions with others. These popular consumer devices are shown in Figure 5.4.

Figure 5.4: Ethel, Amazon Echo Show 10 and the Google Hub

Overcoming Other Disabilities

People who have low vision may be unable to use all the features of smartphones and video devices, but they can benefit from being able to boost the brightness of screens, the magnification possibilities and by changing the colours for improving contrast. However, their independence can be boosted by apps such as:

- TapTapSee – which identifies objects through their photographs
- LookTell – a money reader that identifies notes and coins from various countries

- BeMyEyes – uses a crowd of volunteers to provide remote navigation and identification of objects. This human approach satisfies the need for connection for many people and is perhaps the most successful app for this group.

Those who have dexterity issues can find the large buttons on many telephone devices reassuring, while the button sizes on a smartphone keypad can be expanded, as can all control buttons using apps such as Big Launcher. However, the integration of voice assistants such as Alexa into control systems which has the potential to overcome physical disability issues relating to mobility and dexterity. This trend is accelerating.

People who have speech disorders can use specialist devices known as Augmentative and Alternative Communication (AAC) aids as discussed in our second article. They can also benefit from several downloadable apps for their smartphones or, more likely, their tablet devices as shown in Figure 5.5.

Figure 5.5: TouchChat, Proloquo2Go, TD Snap & iCommunicate apps for Speech Generation

Other apps such as ***Avaz*** enable children on the autistic spectrum to communicate through pictures. Sim*ilarly,* **Look At Me** is a gamified way to improve socialization skills for autistic children. More generally, electronic games can offer positive learning experiences for adults on the autistic spectrum. This will be explained below with reference to Steven, who was introduced in Chapter 2.

Social Media

Social media is an important vehicle for people with any form of disability because it encourages communication, exchange of views and activism. Social media sites potentially increase both employment and leisure opportunities for one of the most traditionally isolated groups in society and is therefore a force for good, providing that users are aware of etiquette and the power to harm others through negative reviews and criticisms of their behaviour, lifestyle, or image.

Figure 5.6 shows some of the most popular platforms, many of which are used by professionals and businesses as well as by the public. Others tend to be used more by younger people, enabling them to make friends and raise their self-esteem by enabling their views to be shared and liked, and passed on to others.

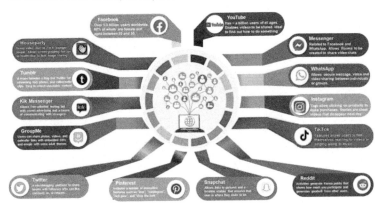

Figure 5.6: Some Features of the More Popular Social Media Sites

There are several benefits of social medial for younger people who have disabilities or other issues that limit their socialising and participation in community groups. These include:

- Collaborative learning enabling them to appreciate different perspectives on popular issues
- Improving digital literacy in a way that encourages rapid use of devices that they might otherwise avoid

- Removing the boundaries associated with meeting and maintaining friendships
- Supporting their mental health and well-being

The potential for on-line abuse is always present in the digital world. Parents and support workers should provide guidance and support to ensure that users are trained in good digital etiquette and given the tools to report inappropriate behaviour. Support service therefore need to include both technical support and friendly advice for staying safe on-line.

Electronic and Computer Games and Sports

Sport is recognised as a force for good. It brings a range of benefits to participants including:

1. Physical health improvement, especially heart fitness and weight control
2. Mental health promotion associated with a healthy body
3. Increased social interaction and participation in teams or partnership, especially when they lead to a sense of achievement
4. The relief of stress
5. Simple enjoyment

Unfortunately, people with disabilities are sometimes unable to participate in competitive sport. The growth in electronic games and eSports offers everyone the chance to join a team and to take part in team events that can produce similar benefits to actual sport – except for the physical activities.

There are now qualifications available, and eSports are being accepted at all levels, including the Olympic Games. They are forms of competition using video gaming consoles or computers enabling multi-player events to be organised, that appeal to both amateurs and professional gamers.

Figure 5.7: Popular Multi-player e-Sports Games

Neglecting shooter and battle games, some of the most popular eSports games are shown in Figure 5.7. Most are electronic versions of actual sports, though players may be replaced by cars or by rockets to offer more speed and features. They are available on many platforms and for games such as football, American football, rugby, tennis, and cricket. The significance of these games is that they enable teams or partnerships to be formed, and for friendship to be developed where participants share a common interest.

Conclusions

Communication and connectedness are essential to our lives. Technology can overcome some of the barriers to communication by addressing sensory and other disabilities, especially when they involve 'Design for All' principles. Everyone's needs are different, so it is essential that an assessment considers the different types of needs (as described in our second article) and avoids the possibility of prescribing standard technologies and applications to everyone.

Social media is the modern way to socialise, and can help bring people together, if they have access to digital devices and have training in their safe use. Similarly, eSports can overcome the need to travel to be with a team, as it allows participation from the comfort and security of someone's personal and favourite space. This can provide a common ground or a strengths-based medium that offers opportunities for striking up conversations. More generally, they provide occupation by keeping minds busy and offering a form of escapism. This is likely to appeal particularly to some people on the Autistic Spectrum or those who suffer from Asperger's syndrome.

Games and social media offer tremendous choices and freedoms that can't always be achieved in the physical world. When matched with individual preferences and needs, they can help people to unwind and relax because they feel in control of their actions. They can become addictive, but their use can also be controlled relatively easily using electronic timers and agreed limits on how long they can be used every day. They are a fundamental part of the 21st Century and are therefore ideal for including in the support package of people with disabilities, if assessed as being appropriate.

In the next chapter, we will consider the role of technology in addressing the safety and security issues that are relevant to people with disabilities.

Chapter 6

Safety and security needs - the role of consumer and bespoke devices

Introduction

We all live with risk. It is an important part of living independently. But while some people are risk averse, others might appear reckless – it is both a matter of individual choice and one of perception. Yet, whenever an accident occurs, the blame culture often comes in to play. We ask what hazards have been identified and whether a risk assessment has been performed. We expect to see reports of what interventions have been implemented to manage or mitigate the risks.

Risk is the product of the likelihood of an incident or accident occurring and the adverse consequences if it does happen. The likelihood can be scored using a numeric scale, usually from 1 (rare or never) through to 5 (frequently or certain). Adverse consequences can range from 1 (inconvenience rather than injury) through to 5 (significant threat to life or limb i.e., catastrophic). Organisations need to take action to reduce high or extreme scores (see Figure 5.1) and to keep people safe – this includes everyone who lives with them, and those who work with them.

| | CONSEQUENCE | | | | |
LIKELIHOOD	Minor	Moderate	Significant	Major	Catastrophic
Almost Certain	Medium	High	Extreme	Extreme	Extreme
Likely	Medium	Medium	High	Extreme	Extreme
Possible	Low	Medium	Medium	High	Extreme
Unlikely	Low	Low	Medium	Medium	High
Rare	Low	Low	Low	Medium	Medium

Figure 6.1: A General Risk Matrix

The problem with this type of risk management strategy is that it can encourage those organisations that are charged with looking after and supporting vulnerable people to wrap them up in cotton wool. This might mean taking away from individuals some of the opportunities to perform activities for themselves and perhaps imposing on them round-the-clock supervision. This sacrifices some of their growth potential in favour of increased safety and security. Holistic assessments can support a more balanced approach, especially when technology can be used to provide an added layer of support that is less intrusive, and which encourages individuals to explore and extend their world of interests. Such an approach can boost interest in performing hobbies and in following interests that improve quality of life and a sense of self-esteem.

For people who have a learning disability, or a mental health issue, there may be a lack of insight regarding risks, it might therefore be necessary to consider different aspects of safety and security so that lighter touch approaches can be considered.

Keeping People Safe and Secure

The holistic approach to support the needs of vulnerable people proposed in the second and third articles in this series provides a platform for identifying not only the risks to independence and well-being but also to the issues and concerns of those around them. To address the promotion of personal security, in its widest sense, we consider the need to keep people safe using the 5 domains shown in Figure 6.2.

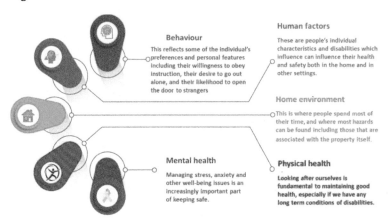

Figure 6.2: Five Domains of Keeping Safe

Behaviour - a good assessment will identify situations that might involve risk behaviour, enabling a range of management strategies to be discussed with the individual. Many traits will be strengths-based; these need to be considered in a personalised way so that the best level of support can be offered.

Human factors – these include sensory loss and impairments that limit an individual's ability to identify risks and to take action to avoid emergencies occurring. Universal design principles applied to some items of consumer electronics overcome these factors, enabling products to be used to safeguard vulnerable people.

The Home Environment – many older properties are full of potential hazards which can result in accidents unless due care and attention are applied. These hazards include steep stairs, dark and poorly ventilated rooms, and poor temperature control.

Physical health – many people have chronic diseases that can significantly reduce quality of life unless they are managed appropriately through medication, good diet and regular exercise. High compliance with advice and prescriptions are good predictors of future health.

Mental health – attention to well-being through talking therapies, mindfulness techniques and good support networks can be vital to maintain mental health in difficult times.

Technologies to Manage Risk

First generation telecare systems that have developed from social alarms over the past 25 years, enable risks to be managed by rapid detection and early intervention. The process is shown in Figure 6.3 and may be relevant both to alarms that are activated by the user, typically by pressing a pendant button or by pulling a cord at the bedside or in the bathroom, or by the action of a smart sensor device. These devices, examples of which are shown in the figure, have been used successfully within system and protocols that use a 24-hour telephone centre to coordinate responses. They are ideally suited to identifying environmental emergencies such as floods, fire, and gas leaks (or blocked flues)., especially for people who live alone.

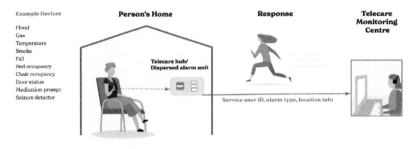

Figure 6.3: An Alarm-based Telecare System

There are three limitations of this approach:

- It is reactive, and therefore unable to prevent accidents through early warning systems and flexible reminders
- They require separate smart sensors to identify each potential emergency
- They rely on the old analogue telephone network and response protocols to provide an appropriate and timely intervention

It is this latter point which restricts the use of such systems for people with a learning disability because they can often rely on a local response from a family member or a support worker. Plesiocare systems that use dedicated pager arrangements are often more appropriate, and do not require the telecommunication networks and therefore avoid the costly replacement of equipment as the UK's systems become all-digital by 2025.

Activity Monitoring and Smart Homes

Many simple sensors can be made smart by applying simple decision rules to them within the device. These are straightforward for many environmental devices including smoke, temperature, and gas level devices. They are programmed to alarm when a threshold has been exceeded. Other sensors are more appropriate for long-term data collection, for subsequent analysis to monitor events and

40

interactions with others, and with their home appliances from bathroom facilities through to oven and kettle use. This is the basis of activity monitoring systems. They range in sophistication from those that only monitor movement patterns through to those that use machine learning to identify changes in activity levels or timings that can be used to provide alerts. Personal dashboards can be created to enable the individual and their families, as well as support workers, managers, and assessors, to provide an early intervention under circumstances such as poor sleep quality, a lack of activity or a failure to prepare food or drink as often as needed.

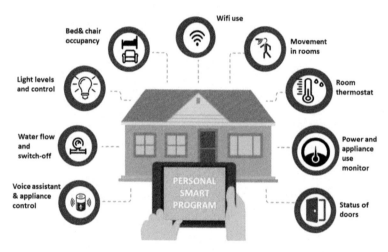

Figure 6.4: Activity Monitoring and Control Sensor and Actuators

The more sensors, the greater the predictive power of the data produced, but also the potential intrusion into the lives of the people being monitored. There is a need for informed consent to ensure that appropriate ethical guidelines are being followed. Activity monitoring systems will soon become so powerful that they will enable remote carers to analyse an individual's domestic routines and identify changes that might include having an overnight guest. Independence means being able to do such things without the fear that personal information is no longer confidential, and that permission is needed for normal human interactions and relationships.

The systems shown in Figure 6.4 include devices for monitoring the environment, and those that monitor the activities of the resident. Both can be personalised, but the former is often the responsibility of the homeowner or the landlord, who can use multi-functional sensors to measure light levels, temperature, air quality and humidity. This allows maintenance work on the boiler and central heating to be performed pro-actively, and for the living conditions to be optimized for the tenant's well-being. Other devices are relevant to social services because they can be used to detect a decline in capabilities or a change in habit. In each case, the devices can now be integrated with smart home controllers, whether thermostatic valves, or individual actuators that can open doors, switch appliances on or off, or provide messaging. Personal voice assistants can be used as the user interface and can directly control electrical appliances. This type of smart home arrangement can be used to offer closed loop support. By controlling devices in line with a smart program, it removes the need to involve a human responder, thus promoting the independence of the user.

Once more, the selection of monitoring devices and systems will depend on individual assessment.

Improving personal health

Many disabled people suffer from long term conditions, especially lung diseases, diabetes, and epilepsy. Most of these conditions can be managed through medication and lifestyle modifications, but only if compliance is monitored and advice offered routinely. Wearable devices have made a significant difference to maintaining personal health. Figure 6.5 shows a range of modern wrist-worn devices that are suitable for people with a disability, as well as for anyone interested in monitoring their physical performance and health parameters.

Figure 6.5: Smart wrist-worn devices to detect or measure blood-pressure, falls, blood oxygen levels, convulsive epileptic seizures and blood glucose levels respectively

They all use a feature phone (i.e., a smart phone and app) to provide continuous or intermittent measurement and detection of relevant parameters. They are currently bespoke sensor devices, but increasingly they will be included on Apple, Galaxy and Fitbit watches, continuing the move towards consumer devices for health. The challenge becomes one of identifying the best product to meet the individual need rather than any product that claims to be useful. This needs a new approach to product comparison and evaluation that will be described in the next article in this series.

This approach will also lead to more self-care applications for mental health generally based on digital therapeutics, smartphone technology and apps. Figure 6.6 shows some exciting new apps and hardware devices that can support mindfulness and well-being. Specifically, they can help overcome stress and anxiety and improve sleep quality, monitoring progress using a smartphone app.

Figure 6.6: Pip, Muse 2, Spire, Beurer and Dodow Digital Therapuetics Devices and Systems

The devices shown in Figures 6.5 and 6.6 may increasingly become common methods for empowering people to improve self-care. They are all used with an app and a smartphone, enabling the right combination of interventions to be offered subject to an individual's holistic needs assessment. Their use needs also to be subject to the approval of the individual, and to their informed consent regarding the collection of data, and the sharing of information and derived conclusions with family members and with professionals. Some systems based on apps require no hardware, including Brain in Hand for people on the autistic spectrum and the Monsenso system which is classified as a medical device widely used in the prevention and treatment of common behavioural disorders.

How Can We Help Georgia to Have the Confidence to Live Independently?

Georgia Is the only child of Ted and Carol Smith who have looked after her carefully as she has grown up. Her learning disability was not a great concern for them and didn't affect their love for Georgia, but her Type 1 diabetes was an issue because of her need to inject with insulin. She also had a poor sense of smell, though her sense of taste was excellent.

They bought her a pony for her 12th birthday but were disappointed that Georgia wasn't interested in learning to ride it or to look after it. All she wanted to do was to cook, bake and decorate cakes. She told them and all her teachers in school that her ambition was to become a Michelin chef and to own and run her own restaurant. This ambition led her to enrol on as many courses related to catering as possible in school and then in college, though she was frustrated that they expected her to wait on tables and to do the washing up rather than spend her time in the kitchen inventing new recipes and trying them out.

Her mother allowed Georgia to experiment at home, though Carol was a little obsessive about cleanliness and the need to clean every bowl and utensil within seconds of her finishing with them. Georgia was not very good at keeping the kitchen and her bedroom clean and tidy. She was also prone to forget about keeping track of the cooking time, especially when she became flustered. She once set fire to a cake while she was trying to mix the ingredients for a filling and for icing. Thereafter, her mother insisted on closely supervising her cooking, which caused Georgia great angst, and made her wish for a kitchen of her own. Georgia offered to redesign her mother's kitchen using a design app that she had mastered on her iPad which she also used for keeping in touch with her friends and with her parents.

After spending 4 years in college, Georgia was being supported to transition to adult services by her local authority and support organisation. Most of her friends had chosen some sort of career, while others had decided that they would like to share a house that a local landlord had developed for them. Although Georgia got on well with her friends, she didn't want to live with them and to share a kitchen with them. She wanted to live on her own in a flat, and to spend her evenings experimenting with her recipes and practising being a pastry chef. She expected to receive lots of visitors, many of whom would be strangers, who would present themselves at her door in the hope of sampling some of her cakes!

She thought that she would be able to live her dream when she was offered a job in a local restaurant. Her assessment identified her ambitions and the need for support in achieving a suitable tenancy, but also found that she also had several safety and security needs that needed to be addressed by her, the local authority, the support organisation, her potential landlord, and her parents:

- Fire prevention and protection
- Managing her diabetes
- Avoiding abuse from visitors who might exploit her naivety
- Keeping her flat clean and tidy

Georgia was fortunate enough to be offered a new apartment, within walking distance of the restaurant where she worked. It was in a scheme that had been commissioned by the local authority through a housing association, and where support would be provided by a specialist not-for-profit organisation that would be responsible for monitoring the progress of the tenants, and for introducing new elements of support if the needs changed. Figure 6.7 shows some of the technology that supports Georgia.

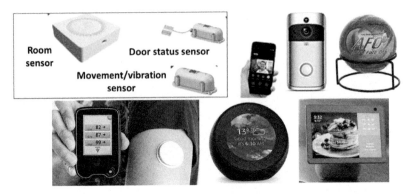

Figure 6.7: The Technologies that Support Georgia's Independence by Keeping Her Safe and Secure

The housing association - it installed fast broadband throughout the scheme, and an Internet of Things arrangement that allowed the environment in the flats to be monitored remotely using a single multi-function sensor in each room. This arrangement allows occupancy, and environmental parameters, including air quality, to be measured continuously and to alert housing officers of any rapid changes that might need attention.

Admission to the scheme is through their 24-hour teleconcierge scheme but with individual tenants, such as Georgia, being encouraged to keep their front doors locked and to use a video doorbell to confirm the identity of visitors before admitting them. The scheme has a full fire protection system in place, which includes sprinklers, though the support organisation would have preferred these to be replaced by Automist arrangements in Georgia's kitchen. She was also provided with an Auto Fire Off fire extinguishing ball which she could easily throw into the kitchen in the event of a fire.

Her parents - they provided Georgia with an iPad and an iPhone so that she could keep in touch with them daily, and so that she could also continue to develop her IT skills through apps and the viewing of professional websites. They also ensured that she was able to benefit from the latest wearable continuous blood glucose monitor. Carol offered to come round to clean once a week, but this offer was rejected by Georgia.

The support organisation - it provided Georgia with 2 Amazon Alexa units, one for her bedside to wake her up in the mornings and to give her a list of events for the day. The other was a larger 'show' device which could be used in the kitchen. It allowed Georgia to make video calls, but also to see recipes that she could try, and to use count-down timers to manage her baking times.

Their specialist technology service provided training and maintenance for all Georgia's devices and systems and ensured that the local authority could be informed of her development and success in living independently. They are currently evaluating new robotic devices that would help Georgia to keep her flat tidy, and a Fingerbot which would enable Georgia to switch on or off any device using Alexa or directly from her iPhone.

Chapter 7

Evaluating Products and Interventions for Addressing the Needs of Vulnerable People

Introduction

Nobody can live a totally independent life. We all need some level of interaction and support to fulfil our hopes and dreams. But people who have a disability may need a little extra help to perform everyday tasks, and to grow and to thrive according to their individual needs. These needs should be identified in an assessment which involves two components. The first involves getting to know the individual so that both their strengths and their weaknesses can be identified. Ideally, their personal strengths, such as their skills, hobbies, and family support (their circle of support) can be enhanced to help them achieve some of their ambitions. These attributes can also play a role in addressing some of their safety, security and communications needs that can challenge their ability to live successfully and independently.

The second part of the assessment requires matching of possible interventions to the needs as a solution that satisfies the individual, and which can be delivered by a service. This can include offering people personal support to learn new skills and, where that isn't possible, performing tasks with them or for them. This is the traditional way of providing support and is like the way that domiciliary care services are often provided for older people who are no longer able to look after themselves at home. These services allow people to continue to live in their own homes, rather than move into residential or nursing homes. However, they are not designed primarily to help people to do more for themselves, nor are they likely to enable people's independent living skills to be restored – though intensive short periods of reablement or enablement are proving to be very useful for people who have recently returned home from hospital.

Community equipment, including walking aids, devices to help people to get up from a chair, a toilet or a bed without help, and special beds, have been very popular in helping people to perform routine domestic activities for many years. More sophisticated equipment such as stair lifts, hoists and adaptations to the home can be equally successful in helping people to overcome mobility or strength issues, and to avoid the need for carers to support them on a day-to-day basis. The scope of such equipment, and Assistive Technologies more generally, is being extended to include more electronic and smart devices, many of which are routinely available and used as consumer devices.

Assistive Technologies (AT)

Any device or system that can help people to perform a task can be assistive. AT is been based on the four pillars of support in Figure 7.1. Most of the home adaptions, portable devices and functional aids are low-tech, mechanical, and easily understood by users; some designs have little visual appeal and can be regarded as stigmatising. However, an increasing number of functional aids are smart in that they use electronics and computing elements and are often smaller and more aesthetically pleasing. All devices and systems collected under the Communications and IT Systems grouping are digital in nature, and therefore more consistent with 21st Century support.

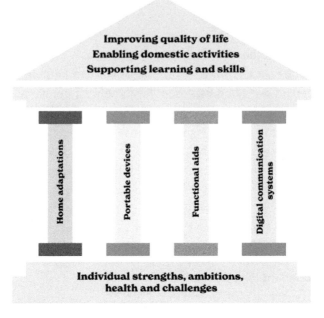

Figure 7.1: The Four Pillars of Assistive Technology Support

Traditional forms of AT are well-known to Occupational Therapists and to other professional staff who are trying to develop a support package for their patients and for those people who need a bit of help to improve their lives.

Table 7.1 shows 27 categories used by the Disabled Living Foundation to describe different forms of AT. In addition to these, there are two categories relating to wheelchairs, one for manual devices and the other for powered devices that include a pavement scooter.

Only four groups – Communications aids, Memory aids, Telecare and Telephones and Intercoms – are included that that might be described as Digital Technology Enabled Care systems. The categories therefore exclude several new developments in soft robots, Virtual and Augmentive Reality, Digital Therapeutics, and the apps that are already transforming support in many areas and for groups with mental health and/or learning disability issues. Thus, the many functional and digital communication aids that have been introduced in recent years are not likely to be known to assessors. Herein lies the challenge to match new devices to the needs of potential users.

Our approach has involved the development of a new assessment tool that enables an individual's needs to be described in terms of the growth and safety/security areas as in the Tree of Life metaphor shown in Chapter 2.

This allows an individual's potential to be described in terms of their strengths and weaknesses, that can be addressed through a blended approach of traditional support and learning, enhanced by lighter touch interventions. These include a focus on assistive technologies, each of which can be considered for their relevance and efficacy in meeting individual needs. We believe that such an approach is new and has the potential to enable assessors to match the needs of people more easily and accurately with the items of assistive technology that are most appropriate, and popular, with them.

Table 7.1: The Disabled Living Foundation Categories of AT

Access aids	Eating/drinking aids	Office furniture and equipment
Bariatric equipment	Footwear	Personal aids for bathing
Beds and accessories	Hearing amplifiers and aids	Personal toilet equipment
Chairs and accessories	Home equipment and control	Pressure relief systems
Children's development aids	Household/kitchen devices	Telecare alarm systems
Children's home equipment	Leisure equipment	Telephones and intercoms
Children's mobility & support	Leisure activities and games	Transport equipment
Clothing (special)	Memory aids	Vision aids and devices
Communication aids	Moving and handling aids	Walking & standing aids

Options for Devices

Most assistive devices are specific and address a well-defined but narrow need. For example, reading glass have lenses that magnify print enabling the eyes of the users to overcome the problem of presbyopia, a refractive error common to people as they get older. Different magnifications are needed for different people, and other types of lens are needed to deal with other vision problems. The same is true with other needs, and entire categories of aids have been created to deal with deficits in hearing, mobility, strength, bathing, feeding, dexterity, cognition, and communication, for example (see Table 7.1).

As most people have many issues, they may need lots of different assistive devices. Because we are all individual, a personalised approach to the use of assistive technology is required. There are few examples where a 'one size fits all' approach can be applied. The result is that every assessment leads to a unique set of needs, priorities and opportunities for using assistive technologies either to make life easier, or to help people to achieve more independence and improve their quality of life. In practice, how well the devices work depends on how well the matching of device and user has been performed, as well as on the usability and relative cost of the devices, and the willingness of the user to make the devices a part of their lives.

The supply of assistive aids has become a big industry with mail-order and Specialist Superstores devoted to a large private market, to supplement items that are provided by the NHS and local authorities through their Community Equipment loan stores.

However, the rapid growth in computing devices, including tablets and smartphones, has enabled the fourth pillar of AT, shown in Figure 1, to become a ubiquitous source of support for all sectors of society. IT devices and systems (such as the Internet) have become generic tools to help everyone to change the way that they live their lives, from on-line purchases, banking, providing entertainment, planning holidays through to researching family trees and current affairs. Lives have been transformed so that people can interact with the world through social media and communicate both by sounds and vision with people anywhere and at any time.

New personal interfaces have been designed, and Internet browsers improved, to overcome the limitations of many disabilities. But the most significant changes have been due to the introduction of apps – small software applications that make use of the technical features of the computing platform, to offer specific support for the user. They are often at their most powerful when used on a smartphone, and when making use of some of the integrated features of these shown in Table 7.2.

The smartphones and tablets that can host the apps are becoming potentially the greatest and most universal examples of assistive technologies. They can be embraced by everyone and should therefore be particularly useful to people who have a disability, as it gives them the same tools to improve their lives as everyone else has.

Table 7.2: Some of the Features and Capabilities of Smartphones

Features	Integrated Sensors & Actuators
Fast processors	Sensitive microphone
Responsive touch-screen colour display	High quality speaker output
Large memory	3 axis accelerometers
Hands-free (loudspeaker) phone function	GPS location and tracking
Use with earphones	Vibration device
Texting with SMS alerts	Mobile phone cell tracking
Familiar Interface options	Magnetometer
Lightweight & always carried	Temperature chip
Open platforms for innovation	Front and rear-facing cameras & video
Designed to work with thousands of apps	Extension battery units
Extended battery life	Non-contact charging
Many budget options	Bluetooth communications (LE)
Universal charging devices	Proximity sensor
Suitable for different modes of operation	Near Field Communications (NFC)
Easy access modes for users with disabilities	Wifi and mobile data use
Screen sharing	Link with smartwatches

Smartphones, and other consumer items of Information Technology, such as fitness trackers and voice assistants open up a new world of applications that are assistive in nature, enabling them to provide alternatives to bespoke assistive technologies, often by repurposing or adapting their original use. The low cost of developing apps means that combinations of smart devices with apps can be used to address specific user needs. This is the basis of digital therapeutic approaches which are likely to be increasingly relevant to the support of people with long term conditions and/or disabilities.

Which Assistive Technologies Best Address the Needs of Vulnerable People?

People with a learning disability may have many needs, and these are often described as complex, meaning that they need more than one or two interventions to address all their assessed needs in a satisfactory way. Some products may be effective in more than one area, while others are very good at addressing a single need. It follows that there may be a need for several devices, or TEC applications, to meet the needs – especially when used in tandem with some support from staff members. It would be naïve to believe that technology alone can provide all the necessary interventions. Hybrid solutions are likely to dominate, giving assessors, and service users and their advocates, opportunities to choose the best combination of interventions, and to change the mix as new applications mature.

The number of new and existing TEC applications on the market has been increasingly rapidly in recent years, both because of the soon-to-be-completed analogue to digital telecommunications change, and because of major improvements in sensors and cloud computing which are making Internet of Things applications viable for large-scale deployment. This complicates the search for the best match and increases the risk of using a sub-optimal combination of technology interventions, which would likely impact on the outcome benefits and on the overall cost of provision. However, it increases the chances of an exact match being possible.

Rather than identify technology solutions with categories (such as Table 6.1), we have chosen to relate them more directly to the needs that they address. Building on the growth and support needs from the Tree of Life metaphor, Table 7.3 describes some types of technology and applications that may be relevant.

Table 7.3: Examples of TEC applications to Address Individual Needs

Primary Needs Group	Secondary Needs Groups	Examples
Purpose	Jobs, Independence	GPS devices, schedulers
Exploration	Activities, knowledge	Video games, browsers
Relationships	Friendships	Video calling groups
Connections	Communications	Smartphones, social media
	Removal of barriers	Broadband, digital devices
Safety and Self-esteem	Improving self-worth	Skills learning platforms
	Keeping safe	Reminder devices, alarms
	Keeping healthy	Vital signs monitors
	Managing risks	Telecare sensors and systems

Some TEC applications shown in Table 7.3 take the form of bespoke designs that have been developed specifically to address one or more needs of a vulnerable user group. They generally have user interfaces and operational characteristics that make them useable by the target audience, but which would be unlikely to appeal to the general population.

On the other hand, there are more generic products which are available through mainstream electronics or IT outlets and which are marketed to the entire population. These devices might be repurposed for an extended range of applications for disabled people who can take advantage of the technical innovations in ways that the designers hadn't considered. However, they are unlikely to exactly match the specific needs that they need to address but can provide some support across a wider range of need categories.

Traditional Assistive Technologies (Pillars 1 to 3 in Figure 7.1) can make life easier for users in hundreds of different ways. Our product evaluation framework identifies the ability of each device to successfully address a spectrum of needs, and measures how well they score from usability to sustainability, and from reliability through to interoperability. It also considers the level of technical support needed to introduce each device, and then to maintain it over subsequent months of use. This contributes to a value-for-money rating. Only those products that achieve our threshold of acceptability are included on the inventory of TEC interventions. This ensures that service users can be guaranteed both the best matches to their needs and that those matches are of the highest quality.

Bespoke AT vs Consumer Devices

Consumer devices are generally less expensive than bespoke devices because they are designed for use by the entire population rather than for a relatively small number of people who have assisted living needs. However, this means that their applications are more generic, and less focused on the specific needs of users, though some repurposing is possible through software modifications or additional app development.

To illustrate this point, we have evaluated 9 assistive devices or systems which include three specialist products, three consumer products, and three products which might appeal to a broad market of older people and those with a cognitive impairment. Their performance, in terms of addressing the secondary needs groups of needs are shown in Figure 7.2. This shows the broad range of benefits that are possible, especially with the consumer products and with telecare devices. In contrast the specialist devices or systems, which included an app, and a robotic toy, benefitted in far more specific ways but with narrower potential.

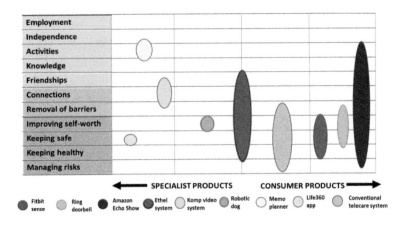

Figure 7.2: The Outcome Benefits of Specialist and Consumer AT Products

Satisfying a complex assortment of needs may need a combination of several interventions, including some bespoke AT devices.

Case Study

John is a 25-year-old young man from Southport who has a learning disability and is on the autistic spectrum. He also has difficulties in walking due to an abnormality in his hips which was not corrected while he was a child. The result is that he struggled in school and made few friends. He lived with his mother and his younger sister, who went to college 4 years ago and who now lives in London. John's mother supports him as well as she can, but his development has been limited by her attitude to risk, especially those relating to computer and video game use. The result is that he remains housebound on most days, and spends his time listening to music or watching sport on TV, though he is also very interested in trains, especially steam trains like the ones that his grandfather used to drive. He is medically well and needs no medication but should be exercising more because of his reduced mobility.

He has been assessed by his local authority and has been allocated a personal budget of £200 per week which he can use to buy services from local support agencies. They will also provide him with an individual payment to cover the purchase of other items of technology that may be relevant to his support package. He wants to be able to use some sort of computing device to communicate with those people that he meets at a day care centre, and to be able to share pictures and films with them, but also to research his hobbies and to find out more about local activities.

Figure 7.3: Ethel, Komp and Amazon Echo Show Video Interface Devices

The support agency has received expert advice that suggests that three products may be suitable for John to use to enable him to make video calls to friends, including his sister, and to share audio and image files with them. They are shown from left to right in Figure 3:

1. Ethel - a large 'always on' tablet device designed specifically for older people, allowing them to stay in touch and to receive reminders for medication and view exercise videos and events on-line.
2. Komp – a simple one button video device from Norway which claimed to be the simplest to operate device that can be used for sending and receiving photos and messages, and for making video calls; and
3. Amazon Echo Show 10 – an Alexa device with a video screen and camera to enable video communication and messaging, as well as to provide answer to questions, and control over electrical appliances and lights through Wi-Fi sockets.

All these devices would be capable of meeting the assessed needs once broadband and Wi-Fi had been installed. John can meet this cost from his personal budget. Figure 2 shows that each of the devices could address some other growth and self-esteem needs, especially Ethel and the Echo device. John was offered a choice and ultimately preferred to invest in the Amazon device because it was something that his friends and sister already used, and which had a lower cost and required no monthly subscription. It also would allow him to access a music library and control other equipment without having to get up from his chair. His support agency had experience of providing initial and on-going training in using the Alexa technology, and were also able to show him and his mother, how to use other skills. He bought additional Echo dot devices for use in his and his mother's bedroom, allowing some messages to be broadcast around the home.

John is planning to learn a foreign language using his Echo Show device and feels more confident to use digital system thanks to the weekly sessions that he enjoys with the technical team from the Support Agency. He receives regular exercise tutorials and has purchased a Fitbit activity monitoring device and a low-cost smartphone to enable him to monitor his improving physiological parameters. His support team are helping him to download apps and to ensure that he understands how to browse safely.

Chapter 8

Developing a Support Service to Optimise the Use of Technology

Introduction

There are many examples of how lives can be improved with technology. Many technology vendors can describe the benefits of adopting their products. But this doesn't mean that this is the best solution for the user, nor does it mean that all their needs have been addressed. The challenge is to find solutions that address all the assessed needs, and which are liked and will be used by the individual.

The assessment process is crucial. Assessment identifies the strength and all the needs of the individual and can lead to solutions that can combine traditional types of support with new 'lighter touch' interventions that include IT and AT equipment.

Assessments should not be isolated events that suggest how life might be improved. Rather, they should be the first components in a service that will ultimately deliver changes and maintain lifestyles that provide continuous benefits to quality of life and well-being.

A focus on service planning and delivery can provide a wrap-around support arrangement that optimizes the potential benefits, based on person-centred principles.

This article describes how such a service can be developed within an existing support organisation, with respect to systems and skills development, training, and selection of technologies.

Service Components

A Technology Enabled Support service for people with a learning disability or a mental health issue could follow a 6-stage process as shown in Figure 8.1.

This begins with the discovery of an individual's strengths, skills, and achievements together with their goals and the barriers that they face. It then moves on to individual issues, risks and concerns. It ends with a review of progress and a reassessment of the needs so that new or alternative interventions may be included in a new support package of solutions.

The service depends on having in place the following elements:

- An assessment methodology for describing the needs in a simple form
- An inventory of appropriate interventions that include both traditional support and an expanded range of evaluated and approved technology applications
- A toolbox of methods to match tools to interventions
- A system of ensuring that ethical considerations have been followed
- A workforce with the skills to procure, install, maintain, demonstrate, and monitor the equipment
- Training programmes to support the workforce in delivering the service

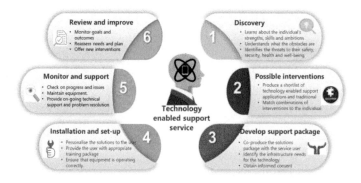

Figure 8.1: The Technology Support Service Elements

Matching Interventions and Needs

The Discovery Process enables the assessor to collect many relevant needs of an individual under the 5 primary groupings described in the Tree of Life metaphor or by the extended 11 secondary group of needs:

A. Providing occupation or employment
B. Increasing sense of independence
C. Discovering more leisure activities
D. Extending personal knowledge
E. Finding more and better friends
F. Making stronger connections
G. Removing the barriers and hurdles limiting development
H. Improving self-worth
I. Keeping safe and secure
J. Maintaining or improving health (and well-being)
K. Managing risks to independence, to the home and to others.

Each of these groups can be expanded into a list of specific needs that can be listed based on previous experience, but also with new and specific concerns that are identified during discovery, or which have been highlighted by relatives or by those close to the individual.

An example of the expanded list for keeping someone safe and secure is shown in Table 7.1. The extended list for each need group forms a database of needs that can be developed and then used by assessors to describe the needs.

Table 8.1: An Extended List of Needs and their Codes for the Keeping Safe and Secure Group

Need Code	Need Description
I-1	Knowing about escape routes
I-2	Remembering to switch off appliances after use
I-3	Being able to make toast safely
I-4	Keeping track of cooking times
I-5	Remembering to close doors and windows
I-6	Not admitting strangers
I-7	Preventing bathroom floods
I-8	Always switching lights on
I-9	Avoiding dangerous streets
I-10	Reporting incidents
I-11	Knowing where you are
I-12	Being careful on stairs (avoiding falls)
I-13	Asking for advice
I-14	Asking for help

The basis of the matching process is to ensure that each possible intervention is evaluated in such a way that they can be described in terms of their appropriateness for addressing each need. By way of example, we have considered nine technology devices as possible interventions. These were introduced in Chapter 8 as representative devices that range from bespoke through to consumer. They are:

- The Fitbit Sense - an advanced fitness tracker (which has Alexa compatibility)
- The Ring Doorbell - a video doorbell and intercom that shows the image of a caller
- The Amazon Echo Show - a voice assistant with video capabilities
- The Ethel System – a large tablet device that can provide reminders and images, and a video communication platform

- The Komp video system – a simple to use dedicated browsing device
- A robotic dog – a companion device
- The Memo Planner – a visual system for schedules and reminders
- The Life360 app – a personal support tool
- A Conventional telecare hub and emergency detection system – with an alarm hub and sensors to detect incidents of fire, flood, poisonous gases and intruders.

These devices were not selected specifically for their relevance to safety and security. Rather, they may be relevant across a range of needs. Their success in addressing the needs shown in Table 8.1 are described in Table 8.2. This enable partial success to be noted, and the potential dependency on other support elements such as automatic fire-fighting equipment, access to a physical response service, or a 24-hour alarm monitoring centre. The need for the training of users is assumed for all interventions, as is the need for ongoing maintenance and intervention in the event of a technical failure of a device or the telecommunications infrastructure on which the systems rely. These underline the importance of providing interventions within a service wrap-around arrangement which manages risks and provides bespoke applications

Table 8.2: The Needs Capabilities Matrix for Interventions to Keep Someone Safe and Secure

Intervention	I1	I2	I3	I4	I5	I6	I7	I8	I9	I10	I11	I12	I13	I14
Fitbit sense														
Ring doorbell														
Echo Show														
Ethel														
Komp														
Robotic dog														
Memo planner														
Life 360														
Telecare alarms														

Items shaded Green show where the technology supports a need, Red shows where it does not, and Amber shows where there might be a possible fit.

Looking at Table 8.2 there are considerably more sections in red than in green, showing that the matching process is complex. It relies on an evaluation being performed for each intervention. This enables each need to be described by a series of Yes, No or maybe characteristics - for each of the categories A to K. This is no trivial matter.

When the number of available interventions is small, the matching can be performed manually. However, as this number increases (as is usually the case for people with a learning disability) a potentially large number of different interventions may be required to address all the assessed needs. The challenge is then to consider each combination of interventions in such a way that the number, or perhaps the cost, and the on-going support, or monthly subscriptions required are minimised. The outcome benefits should also be researched and described so that the overall quality of solutions can also be compared. The final combination of interventions (i.e., the best solution) is decided by the service user.

The selections can be performed mechanically using one or more algorithms to define the preferences and priorities of the service user. Such approaches ultimately may benefit from machine learning and, eventually, artificial intelligence but only when the processes are mature, and the evidence of best outcomes verified.

The Role of Partnerships

The service proposition described in Figure 8.1 is streamlined in terms of the number of service elements and processes, but operation and delivery require both a dedicated team and the development of protocols to deal with the various scenarios on a 24/7 basis.

It is similar in some respects to the old telecare alarm service (Referral to Review) model which has been used for over 20 years by many local authorities to support primarily older people who live alone in the community. However, our service proposition has several important differences:

1. It is not based on alarms, and fixed Alarm Receiving Centres, but on long-term needs and the support of individuals – though some people who have their own tenancies may benefit at times from community response protocols
2. Data collection is the new currency, and its analysis is focused on individual outcomes – these are collected routinely using apps or cloud-platform arrangements
3. The equipment provided does not use a standard hub (c.f. a dispersed alarm unit in a traditional telecare - different but interoperable monitoring systems may be employed, each with their own API
4. Telecommunications use Internet of Things methods rather than the bespoke protocols of a manufacturers and alarm receiving centres
5. Information belongs to the service user – though they may allow it to be shared, as appropriate, with the service and with family and commissioners
6. Success is based on outcomes – these are monitored routinely, and formalized as part of the review process

This results in a self-contained service, but one that can benefit from partnerships at several levels using one or more of the groups shown in Figure 8.2.

Figure 8.2: The Role of Partnerships in Developing an Enhanced Service Delivery Model

Local authorities can play a particularly important role in co-designing and promoting this model, and in establishing standard assessment and review processes. Many adults with a learning disability live in grouped housing owned by a Registered Social Landlord. The management and upkeep of these properties can be enhanced using activity and environmental monitoring systems that can also manage the needs of some, or all, of the service users. There is significant opportunity to improve their respective qualities of life in this way.

Our service model requires an agnostic approach to the procurement and selection of equipment, enabling any tried and tested items to be introduced into the intervention inventory. However, all providers of assistive technology and apps developers can help ensure that their products are considered for inclusion on the service inventory by supporting the evaluation process and driving improvement in the assessment framework.

Other support organisations might also become delivery partners as the service expands and matures. These might include technical specialists who can help with the repurposing of generic products, and with the training of the staff to identify special modifications. Similarly, the service support team may need additional capacity to provide remote support to service users, especially at night or during the weekend, when the service delivery team becomes stretched. Finally, the smooth running of the service might also depend on the support of family, friends and third sector volunteers to relay feedback and provide help with activities.

Conclusions

Our service delivery model based on technology support can become a robust means of delivering alternate ways of satisfying the needs of vulnerable people, especially those who have a learning disability. It is based on a unique form of assessment that aims to match the needs of individuals with evaluated technology-based or other interventions in ways that are both strengths-based and user-centred. The model is an ideal vehicle for promoting partnership working across the statutory and not-for-profit sectors.

In the next chapter, the methodology will be employed to design optimum care packages for 3 individuals with different needs and ambitions.

Chapter 9

Examples Using a New Technology-based Service to Support People with Complex Needs

Introduction

Technology-based interventions can support both the growth needs and the security or safety needs of vulnerable people. The main challenges are:

- Identifying all the needs including the aims and ambitions of the individual
- Matching all those needs with suitable technology applications or traditional support using a strengths-based approach
- Delivering the best outcomes for both service users and commissioners
- Providing solutions within a wrap-around service that ensures quality support, maintenance, training, and the review of outcomes.

In previous chapters we've described these processes, and the development of a service for delivering the support. In this chapter we illustrate how the delivery model could support two different people. The vignettes are not cases studies, and the names employed are not those of actual people. Each combines the attributes of other people to ensure that their individual identities are not evident.

Jessica

She is 26 and lives at home with her parents. She has received extra support since leaving school and college because of her mild learning disabilities and epilepsy. She is prone to suffer seizures occasionally by day, but more often at night. She wants to become more independent and to carry on with her job in the florist shop where she has enjoyed working for the past 6 months. She loves flowers, and enjoys making up bouquets and arrangements, and meeting with brides and other people when they order or collect items from the shop.

Her parents are very protective, and don't want her to have to travel on her own to work every day. She could travel by bus in the morning, and then take a short walk to the shopping centre where the florist shop is situated. But they insist on driving her (though it's out of their way) or paying for her to take a taxi. After work, she sometimes wants to walk home through the park, but they worry that she might become lost, take a fall, or suffer a seizure.

Jessica is digitally literate and wants to become fit and healthy. She has a smartphone and can message her parents and friends without any problem. She knows that she could make more use of her phone; another assistant in the florist shop has shown her how to download apps, but this is frowned on by her parents who think that her support workers should stop her from 'experimenting'. They had a long discussion about her needs and ambitions, and they agreed that her support worker should work with her to help her satisfy her ambitions in a way that provides reassurance to her parents. All agreed that Jessica was now a young woman who needed to live her life with minimum interference, and that she should have the opportunity of finding happiness outside her family circle if necessary. They all could see the potential for using more technology applications following a formal assessment.

JESSICA's GROWTH NEEDS AND AMBITIONS

- To have more independence in her life
- To hold down a job that she enjoys
- To have more opportunity to follow her interests and hobbies
- To learn how to be able to use her personal technology more effectively
- To find friendship and love

JESSICA'S DEFICIT AND SECURITY NEEDS

- To manage her daytime seizures in a safer way
- To manage her nocturnal seizures in as unobtrusive a way as possible
- To travel safely on public transport
- To know and share location details with family and friends.

JESSICA'S SOLUTIONS PLAN

Figure 9.1: Way2b and Inspyre Apps and Smartwatch Combinations

After assessing her goals, the obstacles to her achieving her ambitions, and the safety issues that need to be addressed, Jessica was offered bespoke instruction on IT and on the use of her digital devices. This involved one-to-one sessions initially but with ongoing support or mentoring over the following weeks. She was also provided with a new Galaxy smart watch (insisting that the original black strap was replaced with a pink one) and a new smartphone, together with subscriptions for 2 new products - Way2B, a direction-finding support tool, and the Inspyre app for continuous seizure detection were both installed on her smart watch and smartphone. These are shown in Figure 9.1. They provide an automatic detection of her location and send alerts to her parents if she becomes lost, needs help, or suffers a convulsive seizure.

She was also provided with an AlertIt convulsive seizure detector, which was placed under the mattress on her bed during the night, and a plesiocare wireless pager for her parents in their bedroom (see left of Figure 9.2). This enabled them to relax and to enjoy a good night's sleep, knowing that they would be woken up if Jessica was having a seizure.

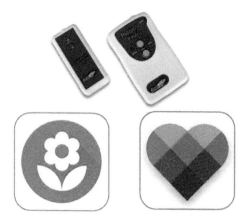

Figure 9.2: The Alert-It Nocturnal Seizure System, and FlowerChecker and eHarmony apps

She also tried several different apps for identifying flowers, and particularly liked FlowerChecker which enabled her to work more efficiently in the Florist shop, and to learn more about the different flowers that she sees in the park. When her colleague subscribed to the eHarmony dating app, Jessica wanted to try it too but was encouraged by her support worker to try smaller sites that were bespoke to people with disabilities. She preferred eHarmony and has been on a date to the cinema with a young teacher at the local horticultural college. She is enjoying her new freedoms.

Robert

He is 38 and has Down's Syndrome. He lived at home with his mother in social housing on the outskirts of Blackpool until she sadly passed away last year during the first wave of Covid-19. He used to have a front-of-house voluntary role in a cake shop and bakery but has been unable to continue since his mother's death and the national lock-down created turmoil in his life. He was assessed by his social worker, who decided that, because he had no living relatives, few prospects for gainful employment, and some underlying health conditions (Type 2 diabetes), that he would be best suited to supported housing.

A placement was found in a shared property on the other side of town. He lived with three other men, all aged over 55. They had 24/7 support from a team of carers who prepared their meals, supervised their bathing, and ensured that they were in their rooms by 10pm every night, and up for breakfast by 8am every morning. He shared few interests with his housemates and felt frustrated at how little he could do for himself. He wasn't allowed to watch late night football shows and films nor to keep his housemates and their support worker awake with his music. He became depressed leading to him being offered a full assessment of needs.

It discovered that Robert had many domestic skills and had been preparing meals and performing other domestic tasks around the home for his mother over many years; he had become quite accomplished as a cook. He would like to work in a restaurant and to live on his own, because he would like to be able to keep himself amused at home without interruption. However, he has few friends and would like to share experiences with people of his own age. He is quite mature but also a little naïve, and needs to be reminded to take his medication, to switch off electrical appliances after using them, to pay attention to his personal hygiene, and to take precautions regarding security.

The assessment also indicated that he was too trusting and would speak with anyone, which is one reason why his mother had restricted his use of a smartphone while she was alive. She didn't allow him to replace it when it was lost, even though he had enough money to buy one and to pay for a good data contract. Although he has also lost his keys and his wallet in the past, he still wants to look after himself, and to take on his own tenancy.

ROBERT'S GROWTH NEEDS AND AMBITIONS

- To find a job and be gainfully employed
- To find and spend more time with friends
- To receive more support to enable him to take more interest in his hobbies
- To learn more IT and digital device skills
- To have his own individual tenancy

ROBERT'S DEFICIT AND SECURITY NEEDS

- To understand the importance of not allowing strangers into his home
- To address safety issues (especially the risk of fire)
- To deal with hygiene issues and to shower daily
- To take better care of personal possessions and to find them when lost
- To prevent potential abuse.

ROBERT'S SOLUTIONS PLAN

Robert bought a new smartphone and was offered intense mentoring to teach him the principles of digital technology. A local restauranteur offered him a position as a kitchen porter and day-release at a college where he quickly developed friendships and learned the value of money. He bought Tile devices; one was attached to his keyring and another placed inside his wallet respectively enabling him to find them over quite a wide range. The tiles could also be used to find his smartphone if he misplaced it. These are shown in Figure 9.3

Figure 9.3: A Samsung Smartphone and Paired Tile Devices

A local housing association offered him a flat close to where he used to live with him mother. When he moved in, he was able to buy his own furniture using a small sum of money that he had inherited from his mother. It also paid for an Amazon Echo Show, and a video doorbell. He was also able to invest in a robotic vacuum cleaner that he could control from his smartphone, and a large TV. He paid monthly for a Sky Sports subscription.

His support worker helped Robert to set up a series of reminders on both his smartphone and his Echo voice assistant device. They also allow him to wake up on time in the morning, to keep in touch with his new friends using social media and through video calls. The video doorbell allows him to see who's at his door before opening it, avoiding the possibility of strangers taking advantage of him. He was also shown how he could raise an emergency call to his support workers using either an app on his smartphone, or by calling for help through "Alexa".

Figure 9.4: A smart TV, Ring Video Doorbell, Amazon Echo Show and Roomba Vacuum Cleaner

The Echo device has been found to keep him amused for hours on end, replaying clips from TV shows and adverts, but also playing any music that he wants to hear repeatedly. Perhaps its greatest success has been in providing him with different recipes to try in the kitchen, and to learn new cooking skills. It provides him with a timer when necessary so that he doesn't burn the cakes. In less than 2 months, it has enabled Robert to keep up-to-date with current affairs and to explore history and many sports. His new devices are shown in Figure 9.4.

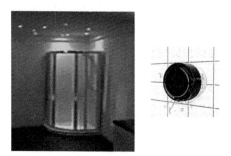

Figure 9.5: Linked Bluetooth Speaker and Colour-Changing Lights in Shower

He has also had a Bluetooth speaker installed in his shower, and a set of colour-changing lights which are controlled by his smartphone and smart home sockets, and which make his daily washing more interesting and rewarding, effectively creating a modern 'disco shower' arrangement. These are shown in Figure 9.5.

Figure 9.6: The MiiCube Environmental Monitoring Sensor and a Water Mist Fire Suppressant

His landlord was also pleased to support his tenancy by fitting the property with an activity and environmental monitoring system that enabled Robert and his support workers to view a dashboard and to receive alerts if there were changes in his habits, or if there were emerging issues in his lifestyle. In addition, the MiiCare system monitored levels of sound, carbon dioxide, temperature, and humidity. See Figure 8.6 (left picture). These could be used to detect unwelcome overnight guests (cuckooing), damp, and the need for gas boiler maintenance. The measurement of sound levels could be used to ensure that he didn't turn up the volume of music too high and disturb the neighbours.

To provide protection against fire, the apartment's smoke and high temperature sensors were connected to a fire panel to provide a direct link to the fire service. In addition, the kitchen was protected by an Aquamist system which, in response to a rapidly increasing temperature, would flood the kitchen with a fog of water droplets; they would suffocate the fire without the water damage associated with sprinklers (see right picture in Figure 9.6). This gave Robert the confidence to further develop his cooking skills and ensure that his employment in the restaurant was made permanent.

Conclusion

Both Jessica and Robert now have individual solutions that include a lot of tech to help them live independently, have a better quality of life, and support their safety and security. An assessment process enabled their needs to be discovered and then matched to novel combinations of technologies and interventions.

The long-term benefits will be considerable and will need to be monitored over future years to ensure the outcomes support their personal goals (which may change over time). The support service will need provide on-going technical support and a review process that can identify new needs and any trends in the use of equipment that might indicate a need for improvement or upgrade.

The potential of digital devices, such as smartphones, continues to grow exponentially and this needs to be reflected in the procurement strategy of the service, and in the training provided to staff. The deployment of technology is more likely to succeed within a wrap-around service rather than by the simple provision of gadgets.

Chapter 10

Capacity, Consent and Ethics of Intrusion and Surveillance

The rapid adoption of digital consumer technologies, such as smartphones, voice assistants, video doorbells and apps has motivated designers and manufacturers to offer more and improved devices and systems to support independence.

Telecare services, based on alarm devices and sensors that are monitored remotely by call centres, have supported millions of older and disabled people to live more confidently in the community for several decades. They have been the platform on which support for people with a learning disability have been built when considering individual tenancies. However, this reactive approach, based on a rapid detection of, and response to, emergency situations is now giving way to more preventive approaches based on continuous monitoring. This has been made possible by the development of:

- Low-cost, miniature sensors, including image-based devices such as cameras, infra-red and microwaves detectors
- Wireless digital transmissions systems
- Cloud-based data collection and analysis systems

Electronic systems that use these developments can survey properties to identify environmental issues early, before they become emergencies. They can also monitor the domestic activities of vulnerable people, their interactions with others, and their physiological parameters. They can provide feedback to the individuals, to suggest to them that they take action to rectify a problem. But they might, alternatively, also inform a third party. This might include family members, professional support workers, a social landlord or, perhaps, data scientists working for a technology or service company.

Each of these groups might have a legitimate interest in the data - but the data belongs to the individual service user, who must both understand the implications of data-sharing and give their explicit consent before it can be collected and viewed by others. This may not be possible for vulnerable people who don't have capacity, raising issues of best interest decisions and ethical frameworks. In practice, capacity is a very subjective word; it is clearly possible for some people to have the capacity to understand some concepts but not to understand their implications. This may be the situation for many thousands of people with a learning disability.

The issues of capacity and informed consent create dilemmas for assessors; they need to advise on the best interventions that will both address all the needs of the service user and which they (the service users) are likely to be happy to accept and use. Clear guidelines may be needed, and access to an extended range of products each of which has been independently evaluated with respective to ethical and performance frameworks. There is little point giving people control to choose their own preferred technology-based interventions and applications if the technology is then used to control them!

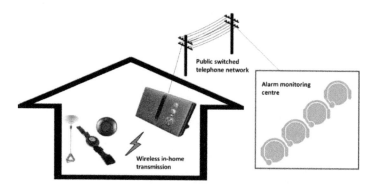

Figure 10.1: A Community Alarm System

Few issues of ethics needed to be considered with the original community alarm systems shown in Figure 10.1, because they were based on active operation of trigger devices such as pendants. The user had control, and could choose to wear and operate the pendant, or to leave it unused in a drawer. But when smart sensors, such as worn fall detectors, were included in the telecare support package, they operated automatically, and the alarm could not be intercepted. It follows that users need to give their consent not only to the use of the devices in their home but also to the protocols of response that will follow in the event of an activation. This may be straightforward for a worn fall detector, for example, but may be more difficult to describe and explain for an exit monitor that effectively combines the information from a sensor that monitors the status of the front door with one that detects movement inside the property. Yet, such systems have been in routine use by people with a learning disability and by people with dementia for over a decade.

It is likely that these first-generation telecare systems will become largely redundant in the future due to the availability of camera-based systems that are low cost and more effective at verifying emergency situations. Figure 10.2 shows a range of low-cost home camera systems (above), which are motion-activated while below there are hidden cameras that allow more discreet surveillance. Their effectiveness has been proved for monitoring pets and the actions of domestic or care staff. They are used by house holders usually without the consent of people in the property whose images may be captured.

Figure 10.2: Remote Cameras Used in the home

Questions that need to be addressed before they are used in properties where vulnerable people live might include:

1. Should cameras be allowed in rooms, such as bathrooms, where individuals should expect privacy, (though many accidents might occur there)?
2. Should residents and/or staff be allowed to physically cover up the cameras to prevent their images being monitored and recorded?
3. Should all cameras have physical shutters than can be used to prevent filming (as can be found on Portal devices and Amazon Echo Show units)?
4. Should landlords have the right to install and view images taken inside or outside their properties without the knowledge of tenants? and
5. Should tenants be allowed to install and monitor their own cameras in their homes without the permission of their landlord and support organisation?

Activity monitoring systems

The replacement of alarm-based telecare systems with Internet of Things arrangements is allowing the prediction of future problems through the intelligent use of data collected with a combination of sensors as described in Figure 10.3. They allow dashboards to be constructed that will provide early warnings of a decline in capabilities or health status, thus allowing early interventions that can help avoid hospitalisation and emergency situations developing.

Figure 10.3: The Five Types of Inputs to An Activity Monitoring System

The price to be paid for this important knowledge is intrusion into the lifestyle, habits, and privacy of the individual. A desire to detect social isolation might also show regular overnight visitors, while environmental monitoring might show high levels of noise, smoke or risky behaviours that are in contravention of a tenancy agreement. The consequences could be eviction. The individual needs to be told about and understand that the data could be used both to help improve safety and security but also to monitor activities.

The systems that are used for activity monitoring are already available and are being introduced by both social landlords (to protect their properties) and by social services as part of their duty of care for vulnerable service users. The potential for abuse is evident.

Advanced technologies will undoubtedly be used increasingly to monitor the health and well-being of older and/or disabled people. They can provide significant value, provided that their use has been fully explained to all stakeholders. For people without capacity, best interest decisions should be made, but with the intention of minimising the ethical issues surrounding their deployment. There are few guidelines in place to cover digital systems, but it may be worthwhile to create a hierarchy of privacy which may place the use of cameras at the very bottom of the list of preferred options

Chapter 11

Reviewing outcomes and a look to the future

So, we come to the end. What are the lessons we've learnt from writing this book?

To avoid rambling, we've assembled our thoughts into two sections.

The first focuses on outcomes for service users. We recommend a review process that can be used by support workers, commissioners and (perhaps mainly) by service users, to provide a record of what they have achieved.

The second section describes some changes that technology will bring over the coming years (and always more quickly than we imagine). What will be the impact on social care, and specifically on people with learning disabilities and the services that support them?

Outcomes Review

Chapter 8 discussed the importance of having in place an end-to-end service that could support the end-user throughout the journey of support. This service might consist of the nine steps shown in Figure 11.1. The assessment process is fundamental at the start of the journey in identifying the needs and preferences of the user. It moves on to finding the most appropriate interventions to address these needs (using the strengths of the user wherever possible) before building a package of care. This solution needs to be appropriate, and agreed with the service user, before being implemented through installation and bespoke training.

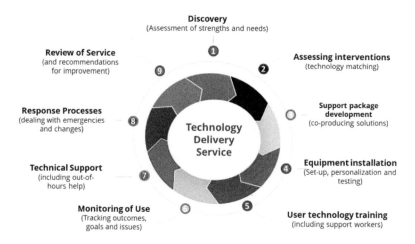

Figure 11.1: A Care and Support Technology Process

Thereafter, both the technology elements and the support elements are monitored on a continual basis, both to ensure that the technology is being used appropriately, and that the system is working well without any technical glitches.

Both technical and human responders may be needed to provide 24-hour support so that the system works when needed, and that there are appropriate interventions available to deal with emergencies. These may be detected automatically using the sensors and the technology platform, or they may be issues that are reported by the service user or their support staff.

Step 9 in the process requires regular review, both to consider general progress, and to identify any devices of technology applications that either aren't working, or which have proved to be unsuitable. This leads to a reassessment of needs, recognizing that they change over time, and a possible introduction of new or different technologies.

The outcomes themselves can be expressed as goals or objectives which can be as straightforward as boiling an egg without help, or as complex as preparing a meal from planning the menu and buying the food, through to clearing away and washing-up.

The most complex ambitions can be split up into several tasks, which themselves involve several skills and experiences. Patience and practice lie at the heart of independent living, and the challenge is often one of defining the steps in a logical order, and then of teaching them to a service user. Appreciation of success at each step is necessary both to build self-confidence and to provide self-esteem.

More significantly, a record of achievements becomes a progress report on the care and improvement plan. The outcomes are perhaps a collection of the many achievements that have been possible during the period of review.

This approach can work in review if such awards are reported and recorded routinely and immediately after completion. Although paper recording is possible, this is inefficient and suffers from all the problems experienced with paper health records that can be misplaced, lost, or damaged. Software, usually in the form of an app, can provide the specific tools for care management tracking and reporting. The need for all support staff and as many service users as possible to be digitally literate is apparent. This means properties having broadband and wifi provision, as well as relevant people having access to their own devices, such as smartphones, tablets, or computers. Initial and on-going training will be needed, together with the technical support shown as stage 7 in the Care and Support Technology Process shown in Figure 11.1.

There are many software products already in use within the care sector. For review, they need to focus on improvements and outcomes, in a way that can be monitored through a digital scale and evidence through tagged events and photographs.

Figure 11.2 shows eight elements that might be included in a service user review. The benefits of such an approach may be considered in terms of the ease of accurate completion (by an individual or by his or her support worker) as well as by the help provided to achieve a high rating at the review point. Ideally, it should be in a format where progress is described both as a journey and as a set of linked stories.

Clear vision
Using assessment process to define a vision of what matters to individual

Articulating goals
Using pictures to make clear the goals based on personal strengths.

Action plan
How new skills will be learned that will lead to achievements on the journey to goals

Activities
The context for learning success performing new tasks.

Review of Journey

Warning flags
Early interventions to provide support if and when things don't go to plan.

Timeline record
Progress on the personal journey towards personal goals

Progress
Perceptions and evidence of how the journey has progressed.

Ratings
Objective measures of the process reflected in a personal score

Figure 11.2: The Elements in a Review of an Individual's Progress or Journey.

Future Technology Impact on Social Care

Social care has been the Cinderella of support services for too long and hasn't received the attention of technology developers in the same way as healthcare.

Fortunately, there are some (usually smaller) companies who focus on digital healthcare applications specifically to support vulnerable people. There are also opportunities to repurpose consumer electronics to manage needs of social care service users, including those people who have a disability.

For brevity, we consider only three groups in this final section:

1. The Internet of Things
2. Soft and social robotics
3. Wearable devices

The Internet of Things

All electronic devices will in future have their own IP (Internet Protocol) address, enabling them to communicate on a machine-to-machine basis with other devices, but also with systems that are visible to and controlled by complex systems.

If a device is likely to break down next week, it will result in a warning message being generated so that maintenance can be applied before the fault appears.

It also allows (or will allow) always-on connectivity throughout neighbourhoods – thus extending the scope of telecare applications to be always available when out and about – thus supporting and encouraging people, including those with disabilities, to get out and about more. Figure 11.3 shows how this might work with an individual's devices connecting him and them to services and information sources of the type shown on the right of the diagram.

It will also offer a low-cost and common platform for multiple applications including mHealth and mCare and will threaten the dominance of existing closed proprietary protocols for telecare platforms in the home (i.e. the way in which devices from a particular manufacturer 'talk' and 'understand' each other – IoT will hopefully force them to use open protocols so products from different manufacturers can work together).

This will eventually lead to true plug and play capabilities between peripherals from multiple manufacturers and different telecare home hubs/dispersed alarm units – allowing a true mix and match approach where the best possible equipment can be selected irrespective of the manufacturer of the home hub used.

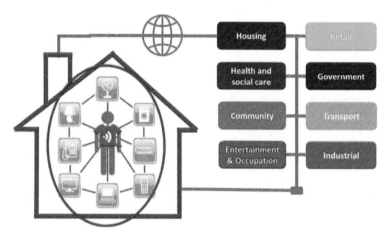

Figure 11.3: An example IoT model

The potential within social care for monitoring and support could be enormous, making safe, independent living a real possibility – provided that the level of intrusion, data-sharing and control are acceptable to the user.

Soft and Social Robotics

The Internet of Things enables devices to interact with actuators to perform standard 'smart home' functions such as switching on lights, opening and closing doors, and controlling water and gas taps. It will also allow more meaningful communication with devices that have intelligence and with devices that can move around and follow someone around the house i.e., a robot.

Voice assistants already play an increasing role in the homes of millions of people, both as an information resource and communication tool, and as an interface to more advanced functions. Imagine an Alexa device that was contained within a portable device or toy – a companion that could be carried around with the user to give them reminders, or which has wheels for autonomous movement.

The robots shown in Figure 11.4 are already available and range from a concierge in an assisted living facility to a linked monitor to support medication compliance. Companion robots aren't designed to replace people, but as technology develops, appropriately designed robotic creature will be able to replicate many of the functions of humans and will be able to communicate and have intelligent conversations with people who live alone.

Figure 11.4: Existing companion robots such as Sam, Jibo, Buddy, Lynx, Pepper and Pillo

The designers realise that robots won't replace human carers and companions, but many see them as playing a similar role to a pet - they are faithful, always available, never refuse, and useful in establishing a routine. The emerging ones shown in Figure 11.5 can offer entertainment, security and safety, as well as an alternative interface for accessing the Internet or making a video call.

Their designs make them suited to roles in service industries, but that also means that they can perform or supervise domestic tasks in the homes of more vulnerable people. The examples shown represent current development across the world including Europe, the USA and Asia.

Figure 11.5: AVi, Aido, Zenbo, Fribo and Cruzr robots

Within a decade, improved battery life, greater dexterity, faster communications (through 5G) and advanced processing will enable soft robots to become viable for use in domestic environments and could become as ubiquitous as a television or computer in everyone's home. Their role would depend on need – so no stigma attached to ownership, because they will fulfil different functions in each home.

Wearable Devices

One of the limitations of digital technologies has been their size, their power needs, and the likelihood of forgetting to take a device when leaving the home. The appearance of laptop computers during the late 1990s, smart phones during the naughties, and tablet devices from 2010 revolutionised and democratized computing.

Nearly all homes in the UK have 2 if not all three types of device. It is hardly surprising that landline telephones, mechanical typewriters, fax machines and pagers have all but disappeared as the new options have made them almost redundant.

The aim of many technologists is to continue the process of miniaturization until we have genuinely wearable computers, smartphones integrated into our clothing, and displays that are components of spectacles. The only questions are:

- How small?
- How soon?
- How acceptable?

Devices could be worn anywhere on the body, but most won't be able to fulfil their function if they are not worn at the site where they are accessible nor if they need to provide some special sensing feature. They might well be smart belts, that can provide location information, smart shoes that guide the wearer to a particular location, and smart shirts that monitor breathing, hear functions and other vital signs – but they are likely to be for specialist applications in healthcare, rather than for the support needed by people who receive social care.

Figure 11.6 shows two of the most likely smart wearables of the future. On the left is the next generation HoloLens device. These systems may become the spectacles of the future, giving personal 'heads-up' information to the wearer. This might be in the form of visual prompts and reminders, but could also accept spoken inputs and requests, (Alexa compatibility) or the running of dedicated apps.

An ear-piece could also add spoken instructions and feedback. Perhaps the most exciting prospects are of adding Virtual Reality (VR) and Augmented Reality (AR) which can be used for gaming, for providing instruction, or for keeping in touch with friends.

Figure 11.6: A Smart Headset and a Future Smartwatch

The second device (on the right) is a smartwatch. Over the past decade, they have developed from fitness trackers that tell the time and measure steps through to full sensing units that can monitor heart rate, breathing rate, sleep quality and skin temperature. Blood pressure measurements will soon become standard, as will be their ability to perform data processing. They can show text messages and provide social media interfaces so well that they will increasingly become smartphones in their own right, overcoming the need to be paired with a smartphone. They will have integrated voice assistants and will offer wireless ear plugs so that personal messages can be relayed to the user without the fear of being overheard by anyone else. They might also include air quality and environmental monitoring capabilities to warn the wearer of fire or dangerously high or low temperatures.

Final words

Predicting the future has always been a dangerous exercise because innovation is rarely the result of inventors sitting down to work out what they can do with the latest technology. The greatest inventions come from repurposing general designs to meet the needs of a different group of people in a different way. However, with a forward view of only five years, it may be apparent that the inventions are already here but have yet to be recognised for their potential in new markets such as social care.

The three groups shown above are quickly emerging in terms of technical capabilities. If the needs of the social care industry are articulated sufficiently well, and are the subject of commercial opportunity, their impact could be rapid. Front-line workers need to be aware of these possibilities, and commissioners need to understand the need to change their funding models and requirements to encourage new models of care.

We hope this book will have helped to stimulate such thinking in local authorities and in the NHS, and in the families of people who have social care needs.

Printed in Great Britain
by Amazon